BILLY 'NIBS' BUCKSHOT
THE COMPLETE WORKS

BILLY 'NIBS' BUCKSHOT
THE COMPLETE WORKS

JOHN GALLAS

CARCANET POETRY

First published in Great Britain in 2024 by
Carcanet
Alliance House, 30 Cross Street
Manchester, M 2   7 A Q
www.carcanet.co.uk

A CIP catalogue record for this book is
available from the British Library.

ISBN 978 1 80017 443 6

Book design by Andrew Latimer, Carcanet
Typesetting by LiteBook Prepress Services
Printed in Great Britain by SRP Ltd, Exeter, Devon

The publisher acknowledges financial
assistance from Arts Council England.

'Everything is like life'.
Mr Omer, *David Copperfield*

1. HIGH

I can't stand flying:

all that scary bouncing round,

the soar, the plummet –

it wears me out. I don't think

I can love you much longer.

2. CALL HOME

I drowned at Kelling.

Sorry I didn't phone you;

it was quite sudden.

By now you'll be six feet high,

rank with unmown weed and wort.

3. SUNDAY

Sunday; mostly fine.

The Gwakos do pilates

under the sallows.

The Adlers drive to Four Square

in matching emerald tracksuits.

4. AFTERNOON TEA

No.8, Owl Road

is so near the Motorway

Ma Pinklin can tell

a cheese sandwich from a scone

at seventy miles an hour.

5. THE FEVER

Can't sleep: much too hot.

But if I go out and walk

where the cockhold grows

will people think I'm a creep,

sighing in my pyjamas?

6. MORNING

When the morning comes,

like drawers of light opening through

the venetian blinds,

it's sad to button your shirt

and watch you look for my socks.

7. THE OLD MAN AND THE BATH WATER

I watch the bath fill.

The leaden water. We have

all gone headlong-grey.

Let's make love for the last time:

my skeleton, your warm tongues.

8. COVERED TRACKS

The wipers slap-slap.

The van slithers down Hog Lane.

The mirrors are blank.

No one will know where I've been:

my tyre-tracks are blotted with snow.

9. LOWESTOFT. MIDDAY.

Lowestoft. Midday.

Two lifeboats leave the harbour

burbling side by side.

Far out, against the world's blue

wallpaper, I watch them part.

10. HOME IMPROVEMENTS

Dear Gretel, don't paint

the ceiling while I'm in Bø.

I can see your teeth,

nut-crackered in a ladder,

swimming in Nordic Sunrise.

11. WAITING

You said 2. It's 5.

8 mochas at Mo's, waiting

in the sun. You said,

'Your nose is peeling'. The world

is a desert without you.

12. CURLY PANCETTA

Curly Pancetta,

we're friends! Trust me, I can split

an apple with my

bare hands: but saying goodbye

to you hurts me to the core.

13. GROWING UP

Dad planted the old

Gnarly-Pine when I was born.

By night the cones sing.

By day the tops reel in mist.

How come it's bigger than me?

14. THE MEANING OF LIFE

Sit mum. Look wise. Frown

in a big book. Collect saws:

Sup up. Sing shit. Piss

on your feet. Fuck everything.

Ah, there's no comparison.

15. THE POWER STATION

Ratcliffe. Steam balloons

off the cooling towers. Across

Remembrance Way it

pales and fades, where shining sleeps

Ralph, the alabaster knight.

16. CATALEPSY

A trumpet winds jazz

somewhere. I can't move, extinct

in the small, dark hours.

Distant scales tickle my ears.

Good. I'm asleep, but not dead.

17. FLOOD DEFENCES

Take my umbrella,

Maurice! Keep to the high ground.

Wear a life-jacket

and two pairs of galoshes.

Hurry home. Keep your tail high!

18. SIGNS

What means this puncture?

Dogs howl in Sutton St. James.

The poplars whatter.

A dark stranger strides the woods.

The rim rattles on the road.

19. THE CORSET FACTORY

The Corset Factory.

Gorse hair in the roof. Windows

weeping old man's beard.

Chap-fallen mouths of front doors

tumble orders of bindweed.

20. NIGHTMOVES

2am. I'm off.

I'd rather hump in the dark

with a fat suitcase

than sleep alone in this blue

motel, sheeted in neon.

21. THE PEAR-TREES

Congratulations!

The pear-trees that you planted

in the side garden

when you first met have reached the

gutters of your bungalow.

22. NIGEL GOODFELLOW

Nigel Goodfellow

went away to die. How he

climbed the fucking fence

I've no idea, but he's gone.

RIP dear thoughtful goat.

23. MUSEUM PIECE

Miss you, Daisy Hill!

No one loves me like you do.

People come and go.

My gold breasts nuzzle the glass.

Opening hours are 10 till 6.

24. WAR

I load the old Colt.

Grevious Pete's waiting for me.

Blam! I'm dead in the

dust. I wake up wearing a

Stetson and spurs. This means War.

25. THE ROOK

A Collingwood Rook

sits up a gum tree and gleams.

I get my phone out.

He hides in the leaves and squawks,

'Noli me tangere, mate!'

26. CHATTER

Nat, don't listen to

the entrepreneurs of love

who, like empty glass,

twist the undivided light

and whisper in common shades.

27. LONG LOVE

There you were. And I

remembered how I loved you

and cried at the end.

You were with somebody else.

A little battered. Ah, *Tess!*

28. A SENSIBLE ARRANGEMENT

Take my Parka, Dan.

Put away your duffel-coat.

It's pouring in Bluff.

How quickly dry the otter;

how long damp the silly sheep.

29. HOPE

What is Hope? It is

a sand-castle, shell-postern'd,

battlemented, topp'd

with paper banners and well

besieged; and bugger the tide.

30. THE WATCH

Amongst the wet feet

of glass towers, the lights change. I

watch the thousands cross

in the rain. Today you are

wearing a yellow parka.

31. REVERIE

I lay on the hill

and chewed a hay-stalk. The clouds

out-compassed, like some

requisition of the sky.

I am tired of great causes.

32. THE VISION

I had your nipples

within my grasp. Oh, dream on!

They fled upon the

crowing of the cock. I woke.

Even ghosts have left my bed.

33. DREAM LOVER

At night I leave the

door a little open and

hurry to my bed

and knock myself out. How else

will I meet my dream lover?

34. THE PICTURES

So I will go to

The Night of the Living Dead

and contemplate the

back of your head in the dark

and drop peanuts at your feet.

35. MR DONNE

Dear John, thy bee-stung

lips, thy fuck-me eyes, thy big

black slouch-hat fill me

with the best intentions. I

intend to write more poems.

36. TEMPORARY REPLACEMENTS

The sweet weeds have died.

The dandelions wither too.

The lawn looks like shit.

But briefly now a host of

butterflies make flowers there.

37. THE VOICE

When I pump up the

old accordion, it hoots

and squeals and sighs with

merry anticipation.

Are you in there, my darling?

38. SOMETHING TO SEA

I wish I lived in

Karamea in a big

house on stilts with a

high window. I would sit there

and stare at the sea all day.

39. THE BEST PLACE FOR A PICNIC IS USUALLY SOMEWHERE ELSE

Dearest, why are we

hiding percy in the lounge

when the moon is high

over the fens, brushing the

rushes with sheets of honey?

40. PLANTING RUE

So here's Rue for you.

'Tis a pretty bush. I dig

in the claggy clay.

With Rue my heart is laden

for many a lightfoot lad.

41. GRASS

Stop the strimmer, Joe.

Raindrops glitter on the grass.

Seeds tinkle like bells.

And anyway my new goat,

Medium Bongo, likes it long.

42. TREPIDATION

You are like lightning

cracking in the shock-lit clouds.

Jumpy and afraid

I scuttle away. But when

the heavens clear, I miss you.

43. EASTERTIDE

I ride at Easter

down Mole Drove. The hawthorn bends

and drifts to the high

cow-parsnip, whose snow-again

makes white winter of the road.

44. A CARAVAN IN THE WOODS

Who knows what he loved.

He seemed content in his old

yellow caravan.

Quiet as a deer. And on

cold days, a thin wave of smoke.

45. AND NOW

Now I sleep alone.

Like a wounded giant felled

in a cold white field.

I hide my head in the hills.

Snow falls softly over it.

46. SHEEP IN WINTER

For Christ's sake, Lynn, let's

get the poor buggers inside.

The fence-wires are sleeved

in ice. The poplars jangle.

Get your fleece on, mate. Let's go.

47. ON COLD

I watch frost spreading

on the hedges. 3 a.m.

A tallow-faced moon.

On the whitening lawn two owls

hold each other in their wings.

48. SUMMERVIEW

Hugglescote's on fire!

From Puck Hill I see the smoke

billowing from rooves

and lawns, sniffed with flesh and blood.

Tiny figures wave white plates.

49. DONNE ENOUGH

Let us be to love.

Sir, are our hearts your earthquakes?

Madam, do our sighs

flatten your rhododendrons?

Storms will still come though we love.

50. AUTUMN

Let's go for a walk

in the park and look at the

dying hydrangeas.

The paths are foggy. Autumn

keeps us close in a shared coat.

51. OBLIGATION

I fell in the pond

because you like water-cress.

It's only fair that

you shut up and stand still while

I dry my pants on your horns.

52. RUN SMOOTH, RUN FREE

The course of true love

is smooth as an angel's arse.

Should you run into

obstacles the chances are

that Heaven is not involved.

53. A SUDDEN CLATTER

When I die for love

and I'm just a skeleton

clinging to the door,

I hope when you hurry by

next my bone-fall gives you pause.

54. DECAY

Do not be misled

concerning the briefness of

our lives. Listen! The

mountains die too, pattering

away in tinkled shale-fall.

55. DECAY TOO

Do not be misled

concerning the briefness of

our lives. Look! The trees

are bare with winter-wither

and new leaves remember not.

56. I PREFER MY CLOCK

I prefer my clock.

A pretty bird sings the hours

from a bosky bower

happily unlike the fat

rapist of the woods. Cuckoo!

57. PERCY'S TANKA

I met a traveller

from an antique land who said

that in the Nefud

there are nine prehistoric

stone cats perfectly preserved.

58. REMAINS OF THE NIGHT

You think I'm stupid

lying here with my toes curled

and a great big grin

sucking a sherbert lemon:

but that's just how you left me.

59. NATURAL OBDURATION

So I tried it on

when we were little monkeys

and oh! ever since.

Now we are old and grey, our

tails curled round different branches.

60. AUTUMN

I like Autumn best.

When the stout blades of Summer

blunt with yellow drowse.

In cold skeins of stripped branches

the mist-birds cry like small flames.

61. WAVES

Break break break, ye waves

of Bacton, that ceaseless are

the very picture

of my love. By which I mean

my tumbling thrill, not his face.

62. LONGING

I long for the thrush.

The high trees behind my house

are empty. Autumn

and stars. I go to the gate.

Silence. I wash my whiskers.

63. TRAVEL AND THE MIND

Are you sad I'm in

Jerilderie. Are you glad

to do what you want.

It's the same moon. Here they make

donuts with Golden Syrup.

64. YUM

Sing on, Pukeko!

Drag Summer back by its ears.

Make it the tenth of

December again, when we

had that Violet Pavlova.

65. FLUTTERBY

The mānuka bobs.

A wee pīwakawaka

perks and zips away

to more promiscuous grub-trees.

Barkdust bursts from the spurned branch.

66. DROWNDED

At half past six I

always think my clock is dead,

so limp the dropt arms

like poor drowned Percy hanging

in the water, tired of time.

67. SLIPROAD

I think Noah has

just reached the M1. A great

flourish-hunt of horns

brays from the defile. Bonnets

flicker faster through the trees.

68. SCENERY

The windows rattle.

My hot-milk pot boils over.

Outside puffins honk

down at the sea-swell, the white

wind in their precarious feet.

69. THIS YEAR

So this year I am

cultivating Shepherds Dick,

which requires patience,

a dab hand (in all weathers)

and buckets of Blood-and-Bone.

70. THE METAPHOR

Some poets say the

sea has no seasons, cf.

the Green Mutables:

I say I shan't be paddling

at Christmas, cf. July.

71. MOON

Elves admire the moon.

Others find it dumb and cold.

Tonight I watch it

light the reed-bed thickets with

lustrous pearl, to see them die.

72. ALONE NATURALLY

You left me last night.

I sat in the bath and ate

crisps. My toothbrush snapped.

Well I hope you find what you're

looking for – probably mice.

73. IT MUST BE ME

I stare at the stars.

These pearly celestial blobs.

Through night mist and cloud

my old eyes wander behind

a rank of polished lenses.

74. TRUDGE

How much further Mowk?

Snow climbs over everything.

Thump thump thump we go.

An old Wauna honks through the

blizzard. I wish I spoke Goose.

75. TRUDGE TOO

How much further Mowk?

Thump thump thump. I guess it's not

a bad idea,

foot-froze and white-weary here,

to fly my heart with a bird.

76. OBSERVATION

South Key Rotary

is fucking carnage. Bump bump

bump round and round we

go like fucking pedaloes.

Pinks watch us from the island.

77. THE 3RD DEGREE

If pillows could talk

I sometimes wonder who could

really be bothered

to interrogate them by

the light of the bedside lamp.

78. MEDIUM WAVE

Oh what is the point

of dying for love? Did the

transistor still sing

after God had completed

the raising of Lazarus?

79. CHEESE

So I stay awake

all night worrying with hope

that I might see you

in my dreams. The moon hangs by

the window like a big cheese.

80. UNFATHOMABLE

Unfathomable!

When your heart melts will I be

washed away, or just

left standing in a puddle?

I wait with my snorkel on.

81. UNGOVERNABLE

Ungovernable!

When your heart ignites will I

be toast, or light up

like a bloody lava-lamp?

Trust me, there will be fireworks.

82. HILLGATE

From here the hedgerows

roll down to Bree across the

careful corduroy

of two farms. In each a tree,

enisled, tears its windy hair.

83. WRITER'S WISH 1

I wish my love was

secret: then I needn't waste

this white canal, whose

frozen top hides the turbid

mouthings of its throttled stream.

84. WRITER'S WISH TOO

I wish your love was

wobbly: then I needn't waste

the bright remonstrance

of these tearing clouds, that shift,

inconstant, with every wind.

85. LIKE

Shall I compare thee

to a Simile? in whose

Ballroom of Romance

the clamouring components

of the world find company.

86. AERY EXPANSION

How long Spring days are

after the storm of Winter.

Now the sun rattles

fatly in a milky sky

and hope haunts the creeping hours.

87. HELPSTON LIGHTS

Let a hundred trains

go by, so we might sit at

this level-crossing

and hold hands according to

the Highway Code 293.

88. WHETHER

A stabbing finger

of lightning shoots down the sky.

But it misses me.

A disappointed grumble

of thunder retreats, and fades.

89. THE OLD SWIMMING POOL

The old swimming pool

looks green. The paint is flaking.

The iron steps shake.

The lane-markers have sagged and

bleached. Has it changed, or have I?

90. ROSES

I asked the Roses

why they stayed so short a time.

They told me someone

had bought them a Mini-Break

and they thought they ought to come.

91. THE END

Shall I be toppled

by Sir Outwith in the field:

or betrayed in my

own chambers by that fickle

Steward Master Malady?

92. PASAJERO

Death got in my car,

sat in the seat beside me

and said, 'Go and buy

that nice caravan, Senor (?).

Hay tiempo'. Thank you, said I.

93. NORFOLK ISLAND

On Norfolk Island

I saw a mad old pine tree

running down a hill

towards the implacable,

vasty-blue of the ocean.

94. THE WATERFALL

Deep in the bush my

secret waterfall falls its

single silver foot:

and here I am a giant,

my head in the tōtara.

95. OR

I am happiest

in winter, when rhetoric

is desolate-dull.

I'm also very fond of

the busy bees of summer.

96. NEW ME

Who could have thought that

I would ever be a tree?

and freed at last from

roaming, wave my clattered arms

in a flurry of red leaves.

97. NOT SUMMER

My sweet winter thoughts

shall not be trampled in the

stampede of Summer,

when the Earth beshits itself

and white is poisoned with green.

98. BONES

Build me a little

ossuary high up on

Stormy Ridge where in

ecstasies with tūīs I

can clonk like a xylophone.

99. MAGIC

Forty thousand Elves,

each with a silver lantern

stuffed with glow-worms,

drift down the night-blue meadows

singing charms against Asthma.

100. ALESSI

I lie in the bath

and eat a Mars Bar. I think

the novelty plug

may not amuse my heirs, who

disapprove of Suicide.

101. HEAPHY TRACK

Rain clatters on the

heaving nikau-umbrellas;

a leaden sea swarms

at the shore; a track winds on

far into the sprindrift. Good.

102. WAVES

Leave the waves alone:

their innocent mechanics

don't deserve to be

the prey of poets counting

their infinities of love.

103. WAVES TOO

How do I love thee?

Let me count the waves: the depth,

the breadth, the light, the level

and the long outnumbering

of need, and passion, and death.

104. TRAMP

A coat of green moss,

a beanie of cold bright sky,

stout boots of shingle -

I'm away, come rain, come shine,

into the well-known unknown.

105. THE PRICE OF FUEL

My diesel comes to

twelve-twenty; which was the time

my school stopped for lunch.

The plowman homeward plods his

weary way, and leaves the world.

106. CLOUDS

In hot places, clouds

are commended by shepherds

for their pretty shade,

which is an admirable view,

because they are never dull.

107. NEW YEAR

Here comes the New Year,

drifting over the mountains,

impenetrable,

in neutral: the storm is up

and all is on the hazard!

108. IN THE SMALL DISTANCE

What bush-fire is this?

The leaves are flying-scarlet;

Whooping Swans like dabs

of ash reel in the cold sky;

the track crackles underfoot.

109. FISKERTON

Yes, I remember

Fiskerton – the name, because

there was a small owl

standing on the platform with

a paper bag on its head.

110. PHILOSOPHY

The apple-blossom

must be tumbling now down the

old shed's shingle roof;

and I sit here at my books

and pretend that it isn't.

111. UP THERE

Pepeketua

sits in his cold mountain stream.

Shadows of speargrass

fence on the windy ripples

where splay-legged spiders ride.

112. CAVE

Hang on mate, I think

there's a wētā on my head.

Piupiu shade the pool.

I lap water in the dark,

nodding my huge antennae.

113. BLACK IS BEST

When I am old I

shall wear black, because it will

stop people thinking

I'm a stupid old loony

with serious ageing issues.

114. THE BROCKEN SPECTRE

The Brockengespenst

is a meteorological

phenomenon that

has nothing to do with Man:

but it makes you ten feet tall.

115. POETICAL EXERCISE 1

Eight spokes of sunlight

glimmer down into the sea:

Her head on a cloud,

the Statue of Liberty

rests from monstrous vigilance.

116. POETICAL EXERCISE TOO

Eight spokes of sunlight

glimmer down into the sea:

Xerxes's chariot

is stuck in the ocean floor;

he rages in thunder-clouds.

117. TO AUTUMN

I walked out to view

the Autumn colours round Launde.

They were beautiful

and I liked them very much,

but I was not in Ode Mode.

118. SET ME TO MUSIC

Set me to music,

Colin! and we'll do a duet.

Tristan! Isolde!

I'll wear a helmet with wings,

you can peck your bell in time.

119. TĀNEKAHA

plip … plop … plip … plop … plip …

the morning dew drops from a

high Tanekaha,

the colour of rust. They say

that one drop would save my soul.

120. LITTLE WANGANUI

Once I fell asleep

in Little Wanganui.

The Spring whitebaiters

swung their nets like giant sails.

My head lay in a pāua.

121. JOHN

John Clare didn't go

abroad; but he did go mad,

which is a bit of

a trip. I piss into an

English hedge, and am content.

122. WHERE O WHERE

Is there a corner

that shit Summer doesn't find?

where mountains still float

on a platter of cold fog,

sweet and thoughtless as ice-cream.

123. SCRATCH

Remember the rooks

screaming in the blackthorn hedge

as I carried you

down the Lane? Havoc! Havoc!

But the vet said you had fleas.

124. REMEMBER THAT NIGHT

Remember that night

we danced on the fairways at

Brancaster Golf Club

to the beat of the North Sea

thinking it was Tír na nÓg.

125. SUMMER SONG

Remember when dad

led us up Mount Robert ridge

through a hall of snow

higher than our heads. I miss

the bright struggle of winter.

126. DON'T BOTHER

Ah! the moon is like -

Nein. Die Mond ist wie der Mond.

Das ist alles. Wir

wollen hineingehn. OK.

Shut the blinds. Have a Mars Bar.

127. DON'T LOOK NOW

This chappie looks old.

Hello old chappie, what's new?

Blots, blotches, blains, scurf,

wrinkles, spots, plooks, patches, lumps,

frumps and frights, says the mirror.

128. CURRENCY

Penny for your thoughts.

Tuppence for your exercise.

Thruppence for your hat.

Sixpence for your panting heart,

and half-a-crown for your soul.

129. SURPRISE!

It seems wrong not to

try and hide my happiness,

but, like melting snow,

my cover breaks with kindness

to reveal its ruby thorns.

130. PHEW

Funny how waiting

in the fucking bastard heat

was even worse than

the fucking disappointment

when the bastard didn't come.

131. THE CURE

I felt a funeral

in my brain. I had a Flake

and it went away.

Come into the garden, Maud,

for the black bat, night, has flown!

132. MATHS

Medium Bongo walks

the circumference of his rope

with studious horn; stops,

and considers the tangent.

My little Pythagoras!

133. AN ACCIDENT

Ow! Ouch! Eek! I fall

upon the thorns of Barney

Gormley's hedge. Lift me

as a wave, a leaf, a cloud,

a helicopter – I bleed!

134. GOOD PHOTO!

Stop sweeping up the

Autumn leaves, mate. Just stand there

a mo. Great. You look

like Joan of Arc just starting

to ignite (painless version).

135. DIVERSITY

Last Spring I grafted

a Neo-Platonic Sage

to a Brutal Thyme:

it looks like an elephant

and smells of Friar's Balsam.

136. LAYERS

The wind blows ripples

through a picture of the moon

laid on a puddle

in a pothole in a lane

near Sutton St. James. That's life.

137. A STORMY DAY

Turning and turning

in the widening beach, Spot

cannot bloody hear

the whistle. Things fall apart.

She gallops into the waves.

138. GONE TOO SOON

It was a good day;

I'm sorry to see it go.

I had a Cheese Drift

and got an e-mail from Nagg,

and now the sun is setting.

139. FRIGHTENING

Spot lies by the fire,

one half-hawed eye half-open.

Out of the ash I

rise with my red hair, and I

eat mice like air. And she's off.

140. BLACK & WHITE

Much harm has been done

by the poetics of Night:

for fright, death, despair

and ignorance may be white.

For me, the dark ends too soon.

141. LIKE THE WORLD

Dear Mr Omer,

do not the grey geese flying

in the misty sky

remind one of letters writ

in ink? Except that they move.

142. WINTER

Now the watchful Hare

sniffs the night. Haws and blackthorns

bleed in the hedgerows.

Nettles rot. The land is bare.

Light seeps from the moon's white round.

143. BY THE FIRE

Me and Spot like rain.

The corrugated-iron roof

rattles merrily

and we can't hear the vampires

coagulating outside.

144. U-TURN

Well I say bugger

the road not taken: it was

probably full of

stingers and trolls with big clubs

and a nasty way with words.

145. KARAMEA BEACH

I'm the first thing here

since it snowed. Superstitious

of perfection, I

walk in the dunes and watch the

white beach unroll beside me.

146. ZZZZZ

On a willow-raft,

your white kimono flying,

you drift along the

chrysanthemum river and

you're a Poet – in your dreams.

147. WEEKEND

O what is the point

of taking you to the beach

when all you do is

slobber and fart in the sand.

I think your job's too stressful.

148. THE FALL

The extremities

of yellow are the Fall's joy:

bilious lime to

blood-tinc't red, they wimble down

like scabs from a shriven soul.

149. THE TRAIN SET

When I was seven

I had a Märklin, a duck,

a station-master,

a milk-maid and, best of all,

a dis-un-de-coupling rail.

150. YAWN

Bugger the Seasons:

round and round and round they go

creaking and groaning

like a clapped-out carousel.

Poets' rate, tuppence a ride.

151. STOP PRETENDING YOU DON'T UNDERSTAND ME WHEN I ASK IF YOU WANT DINNER

O am I speaking

Proto-Optative-Gothic

or does that little

bimbo smile indicate a

wilful preference for Mousing.

152. JOKE

A Scotsman, a horse,

a piece of string, a giraffe,

a man with a dog,

two penguins, a sandwich and

a nun go into a bar.

153. TIME PASSETH

Ham forgave Lettice,

something he wouldn't have done

twenty years ago:

I guess people change their minds

to avoid changing their lives.

154. ART

Art won a goldfish

for completing a STUVA:

he left it to Ham,

along with his shrubbery

and his collection of owls.

155. DATE LINES

Everything comes first

to the good folk of Tonga,

from where it proceeds

west in a Mexican Wave

to the world's less happy lands.

156. BUSHLINE

At Bushline Hut I

always leave the shit-house door

wide open and sit

face to face with the mountains

rising from the lake below.

157. WHAT?

One night in the bush

I heard the whooping chuckle

of a creature that

only exists in the deep

taxonomy of my soul.

158. HM

Is that evening mist

or smoke rising from the rooves

of Bluff? I'm not sure

whether to sing the praises

of Nature or frying-steak.

159. DEAD PUPPET

Rotted with Winter

the thorn-hedge rattles its bones

in the brand-new sun,

shook by things that live again

shouldering into the wind.

160. OOPS

So endeth all Pride:

Dumb and Dumber cut the stone

on Big Wadburn's grave –

moss-slubbed, it says: *Look on My*

Corks ye Nightie and Respire!

161. THE NECESSARY SIMILE

The pines in the wind

are like demented duppies.

No they aren't: I just

had to bag Nature or get

the existential horrors.

162. THE CARVER

Al starts work at six.

She is making Taranga.

Rain brushes the roof.

The buzz-saws at the bush mill

stop at five, and day is done.

163. WINTER GARDEN

Do the trees catch cold?

I watch my silver birches

shiver in the snow

and wait for the first naked

jolt of a branch-snapping sneeze.

164. EXCUSES EXCUSES

Steff comes home from work,

watches some crap on tv

and has a few beers.

His phone winks in the cushions.

Mate, thy wasted Time wastes thee.

165. ON THE TOP OF MAUKĀTUA

O have I mistook

the moaning of midges for

the trepidation

of the spheres? Yup. Thought I'd got

Translated, but just got bit.

166. SALIUS MONACHUS

The Black Hunter Wasp

is a handsome, coppery

little critter with

an iridescent wing-span

of one and a half inches.

167. DIY

Most thou annoying

fifty flits that million ant

forays in fucking

the Autumn me thou night drive

tranquillizers fucking to.

168. BERKELEY

Up on Stormy Ridge

the piwakawaka sings

to the stormy air.

The trees reel. No man is near;

yet he is singing indeed.

169. WOLVES, BY MR MACNEICE

Respect to Louis!

Tides come and go, but I'm not

bloody banging on

about flux and permanence:

I am tired of reflection.

170. PASTORAL

O I love to sit

under a spreading chestnut

and watch the sheep cud

softly in the still high noon

then chase the stupid bastards.

171. NOCTURNE

Tonight I wander

by the noctilucent shore

to see the black swans

towering in their love-rage

slinging flakes of silver light.

172. AUBADE

I am always pleased

when the sun comes up: things seem

fresh and bright again.

But forgive me for doubting

its reliability.

173. SERENADE

Under Nat's window

the muddy flats of samphire

whisper in the dark.

The sill is stacked with scented

candles. The tide is ebbing.

174. LANDSCAPE

I'm singing because

it's Winter in my garden.

Tra la la la la.

No way am I going out

for a piss in this weather.

175. PORTRAIT, BY MORONI

Mr Grumelli

looks very sexy and quite

enormously pink.

Don't betray me, he says to

a tall friend, *or I'll cut you.*

176. ACTION

When I sleep alone

the bed's too big and I ride

like a seagull on

the pillows of an ocean

and the beating tide within.

177. LOVELY GLINTON SPIRE

Lovely Glinton spire

rises like a minaret

in the placid sky.

It is only when you get

closer you can see God's cross.

178. HARRY BALL

In Blatherwycke Yard

sleeps the corpse of Harry Ball.

Perhaps a few bones

are left, unrattled, in this,

the quietest English grave.

179. BALLAD

O what is that sound

of drumming, of drumming, O

what is that sound that

draws near? It is soldiers, dear,

with drums. There they go. Rat-tat.

180. FISH

I caught a wheke.

It was oogly and orange,

then it went grisaille.

I thought it was pretty nice

and I let the bugger go.

181. TWEET TWEET

Colin, who made thee?

Dost thou know who made thee? O

most probably not.

Did She who made the Wombat

make thee? Almost certainly.

182. UP WE GO

If it were not for

gravity, I'd take biscuits

up for all the crows

pitching in the windy pines

and then go on to the stars.

183. FESTO (WITH THANKS TO IAN & VIV AT THE ESPERANTO-ASOCIO DE BRITIO)

Ho Jamie Vardy,

ni amas vin entute!

Dankon por ĉio;

specife tiu brila

golo kontraŭ Liverpol.

184. A GOOD IDEA

In 1420

some Hussite women spread their

dirty nappies on

Sudoměř Field to tangle

the Catholic horsemen. It worked.

185. PADDLE

I wade out deeper.

From somewhere I hear the cry

of a kororā.

The swell tickles my balls.

The moon lights the horizon.

186. BELLS

Ham's a Believer.

He likes to pray when there's bells.

He says it's good vibes.

There aren't many bells in Bluff.

Hāre Rama ding dong ding.

187. FELLINI

There's a block of flats

in *La Dolce Vita* where

somebody gets off

the bus that troubles my heart:

so new, shiny and becalmed.

188. A PASSING THOUGHT OF SIR THOMAS BROWNE

If Reality

Be Such that *Is*, despite ye

Wish or fond Belief

of Man, then what ye fucke is

ye Pond I dream't on last night?

189. ERGANI

I really hate dogs.

Shepherds wait on silent hills

in a frosty mist,

their wide capes slowly swinging.

I see Rabies in their eyes.

190. NOCTURNE TOO

When I walk to Tydd

at night, the drowsy pigeons

clatter off the trees

like a string of jumping-jacks

fired by my moon-flamed eyes.

191. ACROSS THE LAND

The ferry's in safe.

I jump on the old bike and

head for Letterfrac.

Four days later a njogel

swims into Barnaderg Bay.

192. AN ENCOUNTER WITH LOVE

I saw Dan Cupid

buzzing round the black birches

near Tapawera.

I asked him what he doth there:

'Do ye know Nan Spragg?' he piped.

193. WAR & PEACE

The war canoes of

Laufoli churn overhead.

Their dark bellies cleave

the green sky. Swish … ssssh. Now the

sea floods with sunlight again.

194. DNA

Dr Lofty says

Saint Walbert's Finger is a

gorilla's penis.

Deus ne nos inducas

in tentationem amen.

195. THE YEAR'S WATCH

How lovely are the

slow fireworks of trees: the long

explosions of Time;

and all the alteration

fit for patience, and the sky.

196. RUNES

So I'm going to die.

No pain, it says here, just a

dissociation

by degrees then a pale *poof!*

I'm looking forward to that.

197. OH WHAT SHALL WE DO

Oh what shall we do?

Be frightful and multiply.

Oh I shan't, I shan't!

Well then my friend, you are free

to do whatever you want.

198. ENVOI

Mōrena, Colin!

Like a ride on my tanker?

You can sit up top

and whistle down the wind, mate,

while the horn goes boop boop boop!

ACKNOWLEDGEMENTS

With thanks to Mikey, Vaughan R, Suzz & Les, Patti O and Dave & Irene.

A selection of forty tankas was first published by New Walk Editions as *Aotearoa/Angleland*, edited by Nick Everett & Rory Waterman (2021).

INDEX

THE END